PYTHAGORAS

Pioneering Mathematician and Musical Theorist of Ancient Greece

THE LIBRARY OF GREEK PHILOSOPHERS™

PYTHAGORAS

Pioneering Mathematician and Musical Theorist of Ancient Greece

Dimitra Karamanides

The Rosen Publishing Group, Inc., New York

To my mom and dad

Published in 2006 by The Rosen Publishing Group, Inc.
29 East 21st Street, New York, NY 10010

First Edition

Library of Congress Cataloging-in-Publication Data

Karamanides, Dimitra.
Pythagoras: pioneering mathematician and musical theorist of ancient Greece / Dimitra Karamanides.—1st ed.
    p. cm.—(The library of Greek philosophers)
Includes bibliographical references and index.
ISBN 1-4042-0500-4 (lib. bdg.)
1. Pythagoras. 2. Philosophers—Greece—Biography.
I. Title. II. Series.
B243.K37 2005
182'.2—dc22
                                    2005011968

Printed in China

On the cover: Background: A detail of *Pythagoreans' Hymn to the Rising Sun*, an 1869 oil painting by Fedor Andreevich Bronnikov. Inset: An ancient Greek sculpture bust of Pythagoras.

CONTENTS

Introduction   6

1   The Early Years   9

2   The Traveling Student   15

3   Egypt and Babylon   22

4   A Return to Greece   32

5   The Pythagorean School   37

6   Pythagorean Thought   53

7   Pythagoras's Legacy   90

Timeline   100

Glossary   102

For More Information   104

For Further Reading   106

Bibliography   107

Index   109

INTRODUCTION

When most of us think of ancient Greek philosophy, we are likely to call to mind Socrates and his famous pupil, Plato, and Aristotle, who was Plato's student and Alexander the Great's tutor. These philosophers belonged to what we now call Greece's Classical period, which lasted from approximately 500 to 350 BC.

Classical period figures like Socrates, Plato, and Aristotle dominate our concept of ancient Greek thought. Not as recognizable are the thinkers who laid the groundwork for these more well-known philosophers. These thinkers, many of whom lived 200 years before Plato, are called the Pre-Socratics. One of these Pre-Socratics was Pythagoras, a man whose intellectual accomplishments reach far beyond

These ancient paving stones form a path known as the Heraion of Samos, or the Sacred Way. The road, which has existed since at least the early sixth century BC, led from the city of Samos to the sanctuary devoted to Hera. Hera, the goddess of marriage and childbirth, was considered the queen of the Olympian gods and was both the wife and sister of Zeus. The island city of Samos is now known as Pythagoreion, in honor of Pythagoras, its most famous citizen, who was born there.

the Pythagorean theorem for which we remember him today.

Although the exact dates of Pythagoras's life are unknown, historians estimate that he lived between 580 BC and 500 BC. It is difficult to overestimate the impact that he had on subjects ranging from mathematics to music. Today he is most famous for the Pythagorean theorem, but this was only a minor achievement of his teaching. During his lifetime, Pythagoras's pursuit of knowledge ranged across subjects as different as the gods and planets, to numbers, diet, and music. Pythagoras was more than a mathematician; he was also a philosopher, musician, and religious leader.

Pythagoras (seen at left in an ancient Greek bust) seems to have written nothing down, and his teachings were passed down to students orally. As a result, it is difficult to know what ideas, theories, and practices were actually those of Pythagoras and which were formulated by his later followers. Because of this uncertainty, Pythagoras has been characterized in many different ways: as a mathematician, mystic, musical theorist, astronomer, and nutritionist. He is even often described as a charismatic leader of a cultlike community.

Pythagoras consumed all that his age had to offer. He absorbed the physical science of the Ionian philosophers, the mathematics of the Babylonians (in modern-day Iraq), and the mysticism and geometry of the Egyptians. He then created what was in some ways a combination of these different fields of knowledge but was also a new, unified philosophy that was uniquely his own. Most of the evidence scholars have for the details of Pythagoras's early life is based on the accounts of Pythagoreans who lived 700 to 800 years after his death. As a result, some of this biographical information is thought to be inaccurate or legendary by modern scholars. Until a clearer and more accurate picture emerges, however, we are left with the traditional accounts.

1 THE EARLY YEARS

Pythagoras was born in 580 BC on the small island of Samos in the eastern Aegean, the sea that is central to the history and culture of Greece. This area of Greece is sometimes referred to as Ionia and is close to Asia Minor (modern-day western Turkey). Even though Samos is a small island, only about 184 square miles (476 square kilometers), it played an important role in ancient Greek politics and culture.

Pythagoras's mother, Parthenis, was a native of Samos. She came from one of the island's most aristocratic families. Parthenis's family claimed that it could trace its lineage back to the island's founders. Many Samians believed that the island's founders were divine, or godlike, beings. Pythagoras's father, Mnesarchus, was a wealthy merchant of Phoenician

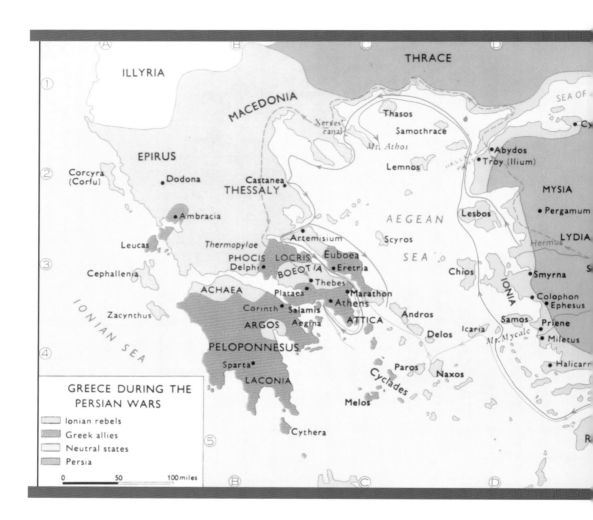

This map shows the territories and city-states of Greece and Asia Minor as they appeared in the sixth century BC, during the lifetime of Pythagoras. This was also the era of the Persian Wars in which the city-state of Athens joined a successful revolt against the Persian Empire and its control of Greek city-states in Asia Minor. As a result, Athens emerged in the fifth century BC as the center of military, political, and cultural power in the Greek world.

PERSIAN CAMPAIGNS AGAINST GREECE

——— Route of fleet under Mardonius 492 B.C.

——— Route of fleet under Datis 490 B.C.

– – – Route of army under Xerxes 480 B.C.

——— Route of fleet under Xerxes 480 B.C.

descent who had settled on Samos. (Phoenicia occupied territory that is now part of Lebanon and Syria.) Mnesarchus was granted Samian citizenship because he provided food for the Samians during a famine. Mnesarchus's business was trade, and he made frequent trips to all the ports around the Mediterranean Sea. As a child, Pythagoras often accompanied his father on these trips. They traveled as far as southern Italy, the place where Pythagoras would eventually establish his famous school.

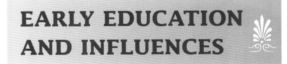

EARLY EDUCATION AND INFLUENCES

Mnesarchus provided his son with every opportunity for excellence. As a child, Pythagoras began what would turn out to be one of the most complete educations that a young Greek during the sixth century BC could expect to receive.

Mnesarchus provided Pythagoras with tutors who taught subjects as varied as philosophy, athletics, music, and painting. Pythagoras traveled to other parts of Greece to study with well-regarded teachers.

Most notable of all Pythagoras's early tutors was Pherecydes of Syros. When Pythagoras was only a teenager, his father sent him to the Greek island of Syros

The fifth-century-BC drinking cup shown above left depicts a school scene. In the cup's center image, the teacher, who is seated, corrects a pupil's writing tablet. An actual writing tablet appears above right. It is a schoolboy's workbook from Egypt, bearing Greek writing.

to study with Pherecydes, who had been initiated into the Temple of Apollo on Delos. Delos was a tiny island in the Aegean Sea that was sacred to Greeks because many believed that the island was the birthplace of Apollo and his sister, the goddess Artemis. People from all parts of the Greek world made pilgrimages to Delos to honor Apollo.

Pherecydes was clearly a strong influence on his young student. Many key points of Pherecydes' philosophy appear later as fundamentals in Pythagoras's own teachings. Pherecydes emphasized the study of music, a subject that would interest Pythagoras for his entire life, becoming one of the cornerstones of Pythagorean philosophy. Also, Pherecydes was one of the first Greeks who taught about the immortality of the soul, specifically that the soul moves from one body to another from one lifetime to the next. Pythagoras preached this concept of the "transmigration of the soul," known today as reincarnation, as a basic tenet of his beliefs.

Perhaps the strongest influence that Pherecydes had on Pythagoras was in his powerful respect for the gods, whom Pherecydes believed deserved study and reverence. In his search for a complete understanding of the natural world, Pherecydes even went so far as to invent new gods who would help explain the workings

A family sacrifices a bull to Asclepius in this marble sculpture from the fifth century BC. Asclepius was the god of medicine and healing. Typical of the ancient Greek world's mingling of mysticism and practical knowledge, people came to shrines devoted to him to have their ailments cured.

of nature and the universe. Pythagoras had a similar mission. Though remembered primarily as a mathematician, it is important to note that all of Pythagoras's theories, even those concerning numbers, were philosophical attempts to bring all things, including humans, into harmony with the gods.

Although Pythagoras traveled widely as a young man, he spent the majority of his youth at Samos. Eventually, however, he decided that it was time to pursue an education abroad. He was only eighteen years old when he set off for Asia Minor to study with some of Greece's most famous philosophers.

THE TRAVELING STUDENT

When Pythagoras set out from Samos to continue his studies, his first stop was Miletus, a Greek community in Asia Minor. Miletus was home to one of the most important philosophical movements of the time, the Ionian school.

THE IONIAN SCHOOL

Only a few miles away from Samos lay the city of Miletus, a thriving port on the Asia Minor mainland. During the second half of the sixth century BC, it was home to Greece's first clearly defined philosophical movement, the Ionian school. It is sometimes also called the Milesian school, after the city around which it grew. The philosophers mainly associated with this school were Thales,

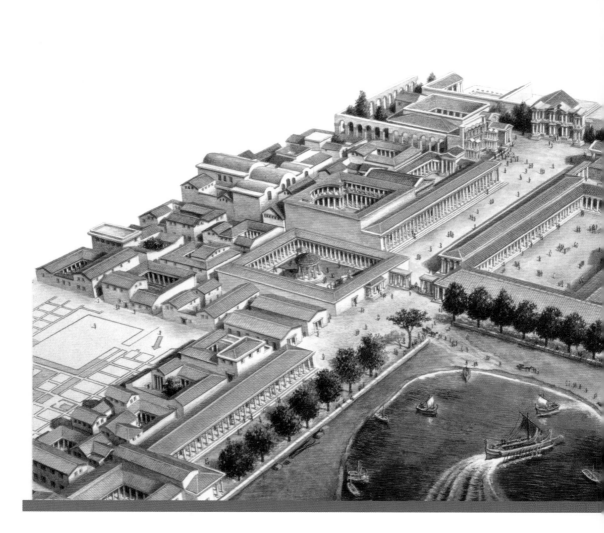

A contemporary watercolor depicts the ancient Greek city of Miletus above. Located on the western coast of modern-day Turkey, Miletus was taken over by Greeks in the tenth century BC and became Ionia, the region of Pythagoras's birthplace. Above right are the ruins of an ancient Greek temple to Apollo in Didyma, Turkey, near what was Miletus.

Anaximander, and Anaximanes. Thales headed the school and served as Anaximander's tutor. During his stay in Miletus, Pythagoras studied with both of these highly respected men.

The most distinctive characteristic of the Milesian philosophical movement was its attempt to explain the world by material means. In other words, its members believed that knowledge of the universe was gained through experience and observation. They stated that humans begin to

understand the world by testing theories, which are carefully plotted and provable. Known as the empirical method today, this is exactly how scientists learn about the world. During the sixth century BC, however, empiricism was a revolutionary idea.

Before the Ionian school of thought gained influence, thinkers explained all natural phenomena—such as rain, wind, sunrise, and sunset—as resulting from the actions of the gods. The behavior of the gods was mysterious, and, therefore, there was no point in people trying to understand the way that the world worked. Thales and his fellow philosophers disagreed. These Ionian philosophers studied subjects ranging from mathematics and engineering to geography and agriculture, to name just a few. They also pursued cosmology—the study of the origin, current state, and future of the universe—and astronomy, which is the study of the movement of bodies in outer space.

According to the Ionian philosophers, all things in the universe were part of a whole. To understand the way things worked, one first needed to find out what the world was made of. Their interest in empiricism may make it seem as if they rejected the existence of gods altogether, but the Ionians' philosophy claimed that the gods were always present in all things. This made it even more valuable to observe nature closely, so that they

could both learn about the natural world through study and witness physical manifestations or signs of the divine all around them. Since they tried to understand how all things in nature worked, these Ionian thinkers became known as the natural philosophers (or *physici* in Greek), meaning "those who study things in nature." They were the first people in Western thought whom we might describe as scientists in a modern sense.

IMPORTANT IONIAN TEACHERS

For a student as curious as Pythagoras, a stop in Miletus to study with these philosophers must have been irresistible. Soon after his arrival in Miletus, Pythagoras became a student of Thales', the Ionian school's founding father. Not only was Thales the founder and leader of the Ionian school, he was also respected throughout the Greek world. More than 100 years later, Plato would list Thales as one of the Seven Sages, a list composed of men whom Plato considered wise beyond all others. Despite Pythagoras's youth, Thales permitted him into the inner circle of associates.

Thales' accomplishments were astonishing for the sixth century BC. He correctly predicted a solar eclipse and was the author of five mathematical theorems. He even used geometry to determine the size of the

The lively debates and free-ranging discussions typical of ancient Greek academies of higher learning are depicted in this nineteenth-century fresco (a painting done on wet plaster) by Gustav Adolph Spangenberg, entitled *The School of Aristotle*. Aristocratic young men attended academies of higher education run by prominent philosophers and teachers who offered lectures in philosophy, mathematics, logic, and rhetoric (the art of speaking and writing effectively). It is likely that Pythagoras benefited from instruction similar to this during his time in Miletus at the Ionian school.

sun and moon. It is not difficult to see why such an impressive thinker would become a major influence on Pythagoras.

While in Miletus, Pythagoras also became a student of the philosopher Anaximander, who had once

studied under Thales. Anaximander's contributions to philosophy included the concept of a universe that is infinite, or unlimited. He was the first person to say that Earth was a free-floating body in space and to draw a map of the world. Anaximander also was responsible for teaching Pythagoras to avoid meat and wine.

Thales' and Anaximander's influence on Pythagoras was undeniable throughout his life and work. From complex concepts related to cosmology and mathematics to ideas as simple as avoiding wine, the Ionian philosophers' teachings left their mark on Pythagoras. It is no surprise that when Thales recommended that Pythagoras continue his studies in Egypt, Pythagoras listened.

Instead of boarding a ship and heading straight for Egypt, however, Pythagoras traveled slowly down the eastern Mediterranean Sea. Along the way, he made stops in Syria and many other lands, familiarizing himself with a variety of thinkers and religious leaders. Pythagoras learned something new wherever he went and added these new ideas to his own developing philosophy.

3 EGYPT AND BABYLON

Thales had studied in Egypt and felt that he had gained much of his knowledge there, as did other famous ancient Greeks, including Solon and Plato. A stop in Egypt was an essential step to a complete education. Thales told Pythagoras that if he wanted to gain wisdom, too, he should leave for Egypt.

During Pythagoras's lifetime, a new scientific age was dawning in Greece. In Egypt, Babylon, and other nations east of Greece, however, similar advances in mathematics, physics, astronomy, and geometry had been made centuries earlier. Greeks considered Egypt to be the birthplace of mathematics. In addition, the Babylonians used what we now call the Pythagorean theorem more than 1,000 years before Pythagoras.

Both Egyptian and Babylonian priests had long observed the night skies and

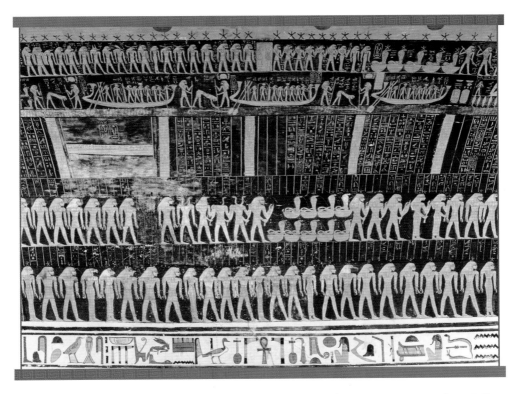

A detail from the painted ceiling of the Tomb of Ramses VI in the Valley of the Kings, Thebes, Egypt, appears above. The scene depicted is from *The Book of the Day*, which describes the daily journey of the sun, from its rising in the east to its setting in the west. Constellations, the hours of the day, and features of cosmography are also represented. Though expressed in terms of myth and legend, these attempts at representing the workings of the sun, moon, stars, and planets demonstrate ancient Egyptians' interest in the cosmos and early contributions to the emerging science of astronomy.

attempted to explain the movement of the planets and stars. In these countries, people used geometry extensively for construction and agricultural purposes. While Greek mathematics was only in its infancy, these nations had been fine-tuning their mathematical and astronomical theories for centuries. For curious

students such as Pythagoras, this "new" knowledge was there just waiting to be absorbed.

EGYPT

Although Pythagoras came to Egypt during the sixth century BC, Egypt's powerful tradition in mathematics

Egyptians were among the first people in the world to use boats to travel on a river. They have been sailing the Nile River for more than 5,000 years, as evidenced by this wall painting (circa 1970 BC). Cargo on ships could include farm produce, livestock, trade goods, and building materials. The boats also transported the bodies of deceased nobles to their burial tombs.

had reached its peak more than 1,000 years earlier. The Egyptians' expertise was in applying mathematics to very practical uses. No other people up to that point had applied mathematics as constructively as the Egyptians had. They used it to create the pyramids, to ease trade with detailed accounting systems, and to measure land. "Geometry" is from the Greek word meaning "the measuring of land." This practice started on the banks of the Nile River, which flooded every year. When the water receded after the annual flood, contours in the land changed and had to be measured again. It is no surprise, then, that the Egyptians were masters of "land counting," or geometry.

Pythagoras studied in Egypt for twenty-two years. Other than the study of geometry, we do not have many specifics about what mathematics Pythagoras learned. However, we know that Pythagoras did a great deal more than study mathematics. He was the first Greek to delve into Egyptian religion, an undertaking that had a profound effect on his philosophies later in life. Perhaps he studied Egyptian religion because the religious centers in Egypt were also the centers for learning. Priests were Egypt's principal scholars. A chance to enter into the Egyptian priesthood must have been an opportunity he relished.

It was not easy for a Greek to be accepted into the long and intensive training of an Egyptian priest. In the end, Pythagoras's seriousness and persistence must have won over Egypt's religious leaders, for Pythagoras did indeed train with Egyptian priests. Before leaving Egypt, Pythagoras was initiated into all four of the country's major religious centers: Memphis, Thebes, Heliopolis, and Hermopolis.

Pythagoras was exposed to a variety of Egyptian ideas during the years he spent in these four Egyptian centers of learning. As a student, he learned about the Egyptian concept of the human soul. According to the Egyptians, the soul evolves and lives on after the death of the body. This idea appeared later in Pythagoras's teachings. He also studied Egyptian astronomy. Crystal-clear Egyptian night skies made this country ideal for stargazing. Egyptian priests were astronomers as well as holy men. While studying with the priests, Pythagoras formed views about the heavens, which later played a central role in Pythagorean thought.

In about 525 BC, the Persians, led by King Cambyses, attacked and overran Egypt. As a result, many Egyptian priests were exiled to Babylon. Pythagoras was one of the priests exiled. Historians do not know many details about Pythagoras's life in Babylon, other than that he spent about twelve years there. The city of Babylon lay

Trained by Egyptian priests in the sixth century BC, Pythagoras studied geometry, astronomy, and religion. Pythagoras's notion of the human soul and its continued existence after the death of the body is probably heavily influenced by his Egyptian masters. The above image is from the Egyptian *Book of the Dead*, a collection of magic spells and formulas related to death and the afterlife. In this image, Anubis, the jackal-headed god of the underworld, leads the dead person to a set of scales, where his soul will be weighed to determine if it can pass on to the realm of the gods.

between the Tigris and Euphrates rivers, in the center of the Persian Empire (modern-day Iran and Iraq).

BABYLON

During his exile in Babylon, Pythagoras studied with the city's priests, known as magi. Just as in Egypt,

The aftermath of the Persians' occupation of Egypt in 525 BC is depicted in this 1841 painting entitled *Cambyses and Psammetich,* by the French artist Jean Adrien Guignet. Cambyses II (seen standing in the shade of the umbrella held over him by a servant) was the son of the Persian emperor Cyrus the Great, who had died in 529 BC during a failed invasion of Egypt. While Cyrus had conquered much of Asia, Cambyses decided to focus on Africa, honoring his father's final failed military effort by launching a successful attack upon Egypt and overthrowing its pharaoh Psammetich III (also called Psammetichus or Psamtik). Egypt remained under Persian rule until 332 BC.

Babylonian religious centers were also the main centers of learning. Pythagoras's studies with the magi focused on subjects ranging from religion and mathematics to music and astrology.

For Pythagoras, a student of philosophy and mathematics, exile in Babylon was actually a lucky turn of events. Like Egypt, Babylon boasted an old and expert

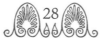

tradition in mathematics. Babylonian mathematics was based on the number 60, a number system borrowed from the Sumerians. Today we use 10 as the base of our numbering system. Historians believe that the Babylonians had been using the so-called Pythagorean theorem more than 1,000 years before Pythagoras came to the city.

Ancient Babylonians were noted for their expertise in the field of astronomy. They were the first people to use arithmetic to predict planetary movement. They were also among the first to try to create an accurate calendar based on the movement of the planets and stars. The magi preserved many of their observations on cuneiform tablets. Cuneiform was an ancient method of writing that involved drawing abstract pictures with reeds on clay tablets.

Although the Babylonians were very successful at charting the movement of heavenly bodies, they were not interested in astronomy for purely scientific purposes. They had a mystical belief that the movement of the planets and stars held the keys to understanding and predicting events on Earth, a concept very similar to what we call astrology today. The Babylonians used their recorded observations to make predictions about the forces of nature, human behavior, and future

A cuneiform tablet created in the seventh century BC, describing the rising times of the planet Venus, appears above. Cuneiform writing consists of wedge-shaped characters, usually inscribed on clay tablets. This tablet is a copy of planetary observations made about 1,000 years earlier. Pythagoras would be the first to discover that what were referred to as the morning star and the evening star are, in fact, the planet Venus.

events. Even the king consulted with astrologers before making important decisions.

The influence that Pythagoras's years in Egypt and Babylon had on him cannot be overestimated. The legendary scholars of these nations gave Pythagoras, the tireless student, enough knowledge to fill several lifetimes. In subjects ranging from mathematics to religion, both countries' scholars provided Pythagoras with an education he could not have hoped to receive in Greece at that time. Finally, after almost forty years of travel and study, he was ready to go home. Pythagoras's many years in the east had finally prepared him to make the transition from student to teacher.

After leaving Babylon, Pythagoras planned to open a school on the island of Samos, his childhood home. Instead of going straight to Samos, however, he traveled widely throughout Greece. Perhaps he did this to catch up on all the latest developments in Greek philosophy and knowledge that he had missed during his years in the East.

THE SEMICIRCLE

Gone for thirty-eight years, Pythagoras finally returned to Samos and wasted no time in setting up his school. The Pythagorean school became known as the Semicircle. Centuries after Pythagoras's death, the people of Samos still held important meetings at the site of this famous school. Pythagoras's school on

Samos focused on two main subjects, philosophy and mathematics. Unfortunately, because the school was short-lived and secretive, historians do not know many details about what Pythagoras taught during these years.

By about 512 BC, Pythagoras had become famous throughout Greece. Many philosophers from all parts

The remains of a circular pedestal from the Heraion of Samos—a temple dedicated to the goddess Hera—are on the island of Pythagoras's birth. The temple to Hera, goddess of marriage and childbirth, may have originated about 1500 BC, when she was perhaps a pre-Olympian fertility goddess.

of Greece came to visit him on his home island. Given his fame and wealthy background, many expected that Pythagoras would live comfortably in Samos. In fact, he sometimes taught and possibly lived alone in a small cave where he spent much of his time contemplating mathematics. After all the years abroad, Pythagoras had not changed much from the eighteen-year-old boy who had set off for Miletus. Like the serious boy who abstained from wine and meat, the famous philosopher still lived simply, avoiding material comforts.

OBSTACLES TO LEARNING

It became clear to Pythagoras that Samos might not be the ideal place for him to establish a school. Although he had become famous, he had some difficulty attracting the type of student that he wanted in the Semicircle. One of the reasons may be that the Greeks of Samos did not accept his teaching methods. Historians describe Pythagoras's teaching method as symbolic and typical of Egyptian teaching methods. This means that numbers did not only represent values for Pythagoras. They also had spiritual meaning. So a question or problem posed by Pythagoras that on its surface seemed mathematical, may in fact have been a question concerning the gods or other spiritual

A community of Pythagoras's followers celebrate the dawn with music in this nineteenth-century painting by the Russian artist Fedor Andreevich Bronnikov, entitled *Pythagoreans' Hymn to the Rising Sun*. Pythagoreans are thought to have worshipped the rising sun, perhaps in celebration of the fresh opportunities for acquiring knowledge and experience that each new day offered. Pythagoras and his followers believed that music could cure disease, and each day began and ended with special songs.

matters. Greeks were used to a more straightforward approach to teaching. Also, the Greeks may simply not have been prepared for the type of mathematics Pythagoras was trying to introduce. Whatever the reasons, there was much resistance to Pythagoras's teachings and his students.

Another factor that persuaded Pythagoras to leave Samos was his inability to focus exclusively on his

teaching. Because the people of Samos held a great respect for Pythagoras, they turned to him for political advice on a regular basis. This was a major drain on his time—time that he wished to devote to studying and teaching. Even worse, as Samos's most famous philosopher, Pythagoras was expected to meet with every important public official who visited the island. Pythagoras wanted to serve his native land, but he did not want to sacrifice his pursuit of knowledge to do so.

It became clear to Pythagoras that Samos was not the place to build the school of his dreams. Life in Samos was simply too distracting and full of public obligations. Like other important philosophers before him, Pythagoras decided he would have to leave his native land in order to establish a great philosophical school. Having made up his mind to leave Samos again, Pythagoras wasted no time. He set sail for Croton, a Greek colony hundreds of miles away from his native island. Pythagoras had visited Croton as a child during one of his father's business trips. In Croton, the most important chapter in Pythagoras's life would begin.

5 THE PYTHAGOREAN SCHOOL

As early as the eighth century BC, Greeks had started to set up colonies in southern Italy and Sicily. By the fifth century BC, southern Italy was home to many powerful Greek colonies. Southern Italy was known as Magna Graecia, meaning "greater Greece." Croton was one of the colonies on Magna Graecia.

Croton (modern-day Crotona, Italy) was established almost 200 years before Pythagoras's arrival. During Pythagoras's time, Croton was at the peak of its power, famed for its medicine and Olympic athletes. Its main source of income was agriculture. Although Croton was far from the distractions of Samos, it was still steeped in the Greek world. Croton's combination of physical remoteness and intellectual connection to Greece made it the ideal location for Pythagoras's new school.

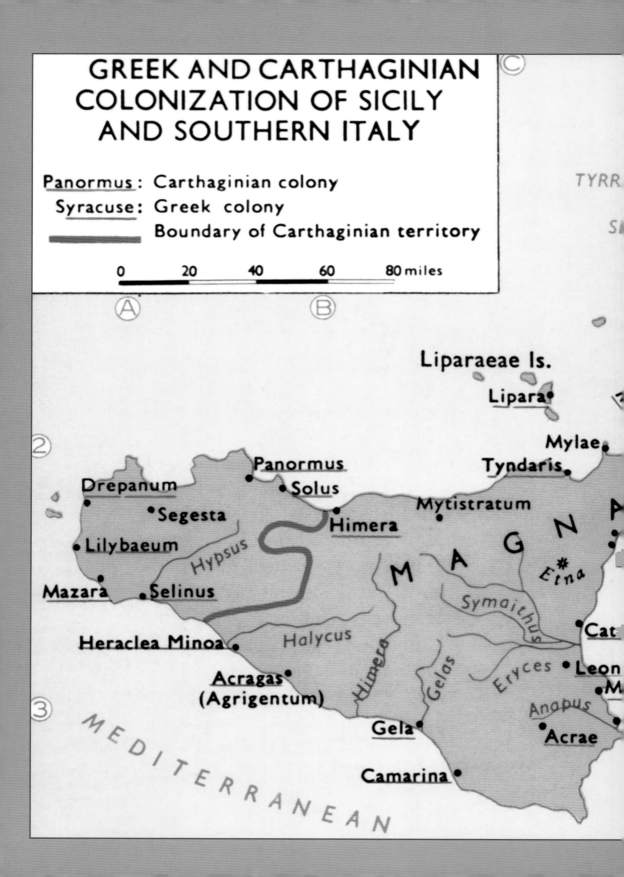

GREEK AND CARTHAGINIAN COLONIZATION OF SICILY AND SOUTHERN ITALY

Panormus : Carthaginian colony
Syracuse : Greek colony
────── Boundary of Carthaginian territory

0   20   40   60   80 miles

Ⓒ

TYRR

SI

Liparaeae Is.

Lipara

Mylae

Tyndaris

Panormus

Solus

Drepanum

Segesta

Mytistratum

Himera

MAGNA

Lilybaeum

Hypsus

Etna

Symaithus

Mazara

Selinus

Cat

Heraclea Minoa

Halycus

Eryces

Leon

Acragas
(Agrigentum)

Himera

Gelas

M

Anapus

Gela

Acrae

MEDITERRANEAN

Camarina

Ⓐ   Ⓑ

②

③

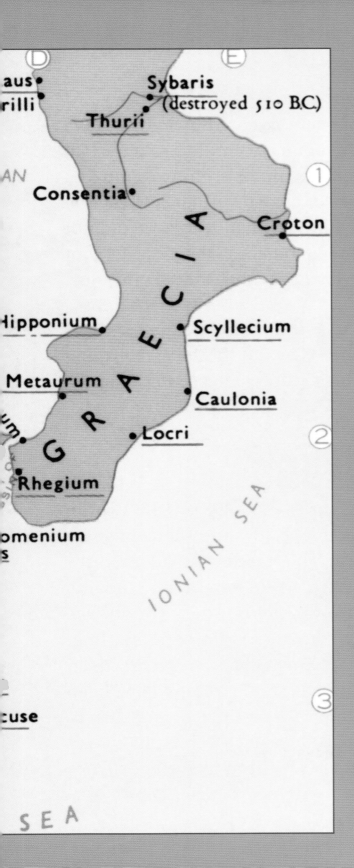

aus•
rilli•

Sybaris•
(destroyed 510 B.C.)

Thurii

Consentia•

Croton•

G R A E C I A

Hipponium•

Scyllecium•

Metaurum•

Caulonia•

Locri•

Rhegium•

omenium
s

IONIAN SEA

cuse

SEA

AN

D
E

①

②

③

Pythagoras traveled to the Greek
colony of Croton in modern-day
southern Italy toward the end of
the sixth century BC to establish
his mathematical, philosophical, and mystical community and
school. Greek colonization of
what became southern Italy and
Sicily began in the eighth century BC, and began to come to
an end in the sixth. Colonists
left Greece in order to find
greater trade opportunities, to
gain farm land (which was
becoming scarce in Greece),
and to escape political conflict.
Greek colonies reached as far as
modern-day Egypt, Libya, Turkey, Romania, and France.

The people of Croton were honored by Pythagoras's decision to call their city home. According to tradition, when Pythagoras arrived by ship in Croton around 510 BC, the harbor's shore was crowded with people eagerly waiting to see and hear the wise man speak. He did not disappoint them. From the moment Pythagoras set foot on Croton, the colony was never the same. Pythagoras and his new followers, many of whom were local leaders, influenced everything from Croton's politics and economy to its family life. They did this by establishing a school that became much more than a center of learning; for many, it provided an entire way of life.

THE SCHOOL AT CROTON

The school that Pythagoras established on Croton would become his principal legacy and the vehicle by which his philosophical and mathematical theories would spread in the future. At its height, its students numbered approximately 2,500. The school was shrouded in secrecy during Pythagoras's time, because he believed that knowledge was dangerous in the hands of the uninitiated. Yet historians have been able to learn about some of its practices and teachings. Not until almost 100 years after Pythagoras's death did a few followers finally drop the veil of silence

that covered Pythagorean learning by revealing the school's complex inner workings.

The emphasis Pythagoras placed on secrecy led the society to adopt very complex and indirect teaching methods. Lessons were anything but straightforward. All knowledge was encoded in stories and sayings that often had little to do with the actual information being taught. The purpose of teaching through the use of parables, sayings, and codes was to keep information out of the hands of the uninitiated. Egypt's influence on Pythagoras was again apparent. Egyptian priests had been transmitting

Pythagoras (the central figure gesturing at right) teaches his followers on Croton. Both men and women were welcome to join the society. The inner circle of followers lived communally, giving up their personal possessions, including homes, and followed Pythagoras's strict rules for living, including a vegetarian diet. The community's core beliefs were that all reality was mathematical in nature, philosophy could purify the soul and help it commune with the divine, and that certain symbols, including numbers, had a deeper mystical meaning.

Miracles and Myths

Many ancient sources tell us that Pythagoras was not only divine but also capable of performing miracles. Indeed, most of his followers believed him to be the god Apollo. Some authors claimed that Pythagoras had a thigh made of solid gold and that he could communicate with animals. According to tradition, Pythagoras confronted a wild bear that had been damaging property and threatening people. After Pythagoras reasoned with the animal, it quietly walked away and never bothered anybody again. Another skill Pythagoras was said to have had was the ability to be in two places at the same time. His followers believed that on the same day, he taught students in Metapontum, Italy, and Tauromenium, Sicily, two localities separated by about 200 miles (322 km). Some believed, too, that Pythagoras was capable of predicting earthquakes and calming rough winds.

information symbolically for centuries, in the hope of keeping it hidden from ordinary people.

MATHEMATIKOI AND AKOUSMATIKOI

The Pythagorean society was not a school open only to young men, as was typical at the time. It

admitted people of any age and gender, many of whom lived in the school full-time. These full-time, core students, who numbered about 500, were known as *mathematikoi*. The students were not permitted to marry and could not own anything privately. When their initiation into the school began, they had to turn all private possessions over to the society. The students lived communally with the other mathematikoi and were no longer allowed to eat meat. The mathematikoi were more than students—they were also Pythagoras's devoted disciples.

The other 2,000 students who made up the rest of the society were known as *akousmatikoi*, which means "listeners" in Greek. These students were given this name because, unlike the mathematikoi, they were not permitted to see Pythagoras, who gave his lectures to them from behind a veil. They were permitted to live with their families in their own homes and retain their private property. They were also allowed to eat meat. The akousmatikoi paid a price for living under a looser set of rules. Unlike the mathematikoi, the akousmatikoi were not permitted to learn Pythagoras's most sacred teachings, including high-level mathematics.

A mid-thirteenth-century illustration depicts Pythagoras at his writing table. The illustration, by Matthew Paris, appears in a manuscript that discusses fortune-telling. Pythagoras believed that individual numbers had both unique personalities and larger mystical meanings. Because of this, he eventually became associated with numerology—the study of the hidden meaning of numbers—and fortune-telling with numbered cards.

THE MAKING OF A DISCIPLE

Pythagoras had many willing students on Croton, but he did not believe that every person was qualified to be given the knowledge that he possessed. Only a select few had the qualifications that Pythagoras was looking for in mathematikoi. According to Pythagoras, gaining knowledge was an attempt on the part of men and women to come closer to the gods. He believed that the soul developed from one lifetime to the next until it reached a divine level. In order to reach this level, one had to be prepared to devote one's life completely to the pursuit of knowledge. Pythagoras was not just looking for students; he was finding disciples. To that end, Pythagoras created a rigorous qualification process that all potential mathematikoi had to endure.

Before a student began his or her training in the Pythagorean society, he or she had to pass a personality test of sorts conducted by Pythagoras himself. In order to assess the student's likelihood of success, Pythagoras looked at how the student spoke and laughed and how the student spent his or her free time. He also studied what made the student happy or sad. The potential student's relationships to family and friends were also carefully noted. Even body

This red-figured drinking cup, known as a *kylix*, was made around 480 BC. The pair of figures represents a teacher instructing a pupil in the playing of an *aulos*, a musical instrument similar to a recorder or flute. The aulos was considered to be an instrument of healing. Given Pythagoras's notions about the relationship between music, celestial harmony, and health, the aulos was no doubt an important part of the daily rituals and practices of the Croton community.

language was studied and analyzed during the selection process. Finally, Pythagoras tested potential students for memory and the ability to learn.

If a student was lucky enough to make it through this screening process, he or she would then be required to give up all personal possessions and enter the school on a full-time basis. The novice student was required to take a five-year vow of silence. Pythagoras considered silence essential to learning. Perhaps his many years as a student in Egypt had taught him that. Pythagoras believed that if a person was able to endure five years of complete silence, he or she clearly demonstrated a

willingness and ability to learn. And learning, after all, was the sole focus of this society.

Once a Pythagorean disciple passed all of the master's tests and was admitted into the community on a full-time basis, he or she concentrated on one area of study, depending on his or her interests and abilities. Subjects ranged from music and medicine to mathematics. The students were expected to excel in their chosen field, and many did. Some historians claim that some of the theories attributed to Pythagoras were, in fact, the work of his gifted students.

A student was required to learn well and quickly, but not all students were able to meet Pythagoras's high standards. The consequences were harsh for students who failed. In addition to being expelled immediately from the school, Pythagoras and the other students would shun the failed student for the rest of his or her life. The Pythagorean society would set up a monument to the failed student, as if he or she had passed away and no longer existed. When other students met the expelled student on the street, they pretended that he or she was not there. It was perhaps little consolation to those who failed that they received twice the value of whatever money or possessions they had brought with them into the society.

A WAY OF LIFE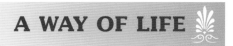

Pythagoras's school offered a great deal more to its students than just the study of mathematics and philosophy. For the initiated, it provided an all-encompassing guide for living, governing every daily action, from diet and sleep schedules to worship and social interaction among students. Pythagoras believed that the way one lived played a crucial role in one's ability to learn. A Pythagorean disciple had to live a pure life in order to follow the path toward a divine soul. The quest for a pure life started by following the rules that Pythagoras considered essential for all of his disciples. These included communal possessions, harmony between friends and family members, worship of the gods, honoring of the dead, fair and good government, a dedicated pursuit of knowledge, silence, and moderation in all things.

The Pythagoreans did not live poorly, but they did live simply. In the words of Iamblichus, a third century AD Pythagorean, "A temple, indeed, should be adorned with gifts, but the soul with disciplines." Pythagoreans shared all physical possessions including money, property, and clothing. Comfort was the ideal, but luxury was considered sinful. Moderation in all things was the goal for which they strived. Students were urged to

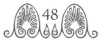

Pythagoras frowned upon drinking wine, thinking it harmed judgment and learning, and polluted the soul. Yet wine was part of daily life for most Greeks. It was served at most meals and used in religious ceremonies, often as an offering to the gods. Not all Greeks saw wine as the enemy of learning. Aristocratic men often attended banquets known as symposia, like the one depicted above on a fifth-century-BC cup. These were wine parties that featured serious discussions of general topics or a specific issue.

listen carefully and to speak only when necessary. Even emotions that were too extreme were frowned upon. A student was encouraged to keep his or her desires and appetites in check.

According to the Pythagoreans, a healthy body made for a healthy mind. As a result, the society in Croton had strict rules governing its students' diet.

For reasons that are not clear to us today, all Pythagoreans were banned from eating beans of any sort. Some historians believe that this was a practice that Pythagoras adopted during his years in Egypt. Also, the mathematikoi were barred completely from eating meat, while the akousmatikoi were permitted only small quantities. Even the akousmatikoi, however, were not allowed to eat the brain or heart of an animal. The restrictions on meat eating make sense in light of the fact that Pythagoras believed that souls migrate from one creature to another. According to Pythagoras, the soul of a dead friend might be living in the body of the animal you intend to eat.

The society also restricted wine, a staple of the ancient Greek diet. According to some historians, the mathematikoi were not permitted any wine except that which was necessary for worshipping the gods. Akousmatikoi, since they were the more casual students, were allowed to drink wine in moderation. Drunkenness of any sort was completely unacceptable. The Pythagorean society specifically discouraged pregnant women from drinking alcohol, just as our doctors do today.

For his initiates, Pythagoras also prescribed specific ways to interact with friends and family. The basic rule was kindness and respect between all parties.

Friends were encouraged to treat each other respect-fully. Pythagoras himself was supposed to have said, "My friend is my other self." In the event that two friends fought, the younger of the two was expected to apologize to the elder. Families were encouraged to

A Day in the Life of a Pythagorean Disciple

Considering how little we know about some Pythagorean teachings, it is remarkable how much we know about the society members' day-to-day life. Disciples who lived full-time at Pythagoras's school experienced a regimented daily routine, beginning with lying in bed and thinking about the previous day's events, then mentally planning the day ahead. Once out of bed, a Pythagorean took a solitary walk, followed by social-izing with others and making offerings to the gods at the temple. Initiates then went to the gymnasium for exercise. Afterward, they ate lunch, which consisted of bread and honey. Then, they took another walk, this time in groups of two or three, in which they discussed les-sons. Baths came next. At night, students gathered in groups of about ten for dinner. The mealtime included readings, socializing, and reli-gious rituals. Finally, students were encouraged to recall the day's events before falling asleep. Pythagoras encouraged this habit, as he believed that it enhanced memory, a capability that was crucial if a student was to be able to learn his complex and coded lessons.

live together harmoniously. Men and women were expected to choose their mates carefully and be faithful to one another. Pythagoras reasoned that more children meant that there would be more people to worship the gods, so students were encouraged to have children.

PYTHAGORAS BEGINS A FAMILY

Following his own advice, Pythagoras, who was at least in his early sixties, married a woman named Theano, who was the daughter of one of Pythagoras's close disciples. Pythagoras and Theano had two sons, Mnesarchus (named after Pythagoras's father) and Telauges, and a daughter named Damo. After Pythagoras's death, Mnesarchus became the leader of the school.

6 PYTHAGOREAN THOUGHT

We know surprisingly little about what Pythagoras actually taught in his school. The school's secrecy has made understanding Pythagorean teaching something of a scavenger hunt. Historians have pieced together information from the writings and teachings of the Pythagoreans who lived at least one generation after their master's death. Yet even with that information, it is difficult to say which teachings were Pythagoras's, which ones came from his Croton disciples, and which were those of the Pythagoreans who lived well after the community on Croton had ceased to exist.

Despite the limited primary sources available, the fundamentals of Pythagorean thought have survived through the centuries. To the Pythagoreans, all knowledge was broken down into four categories: arithmetic, music, geometry, and philosophy. The first, arithmetic, was the study of mathematics. The second was music and harmony. The third was geometry, which included the study of the heavens, namely, cosmology and astronomy. The fourth and final area of study was philosophy.

It is important to keep in mind that in the ancient world, these four categories were not distinct areas of study. At almost every turn, these fields of study overlapped and often blended together. For example, the Pythagoreans' study of music was central to their study of geometry. Mathematics and religion were also a part of their musical and astronomical theories, as we will see. Keeping this in mind, it is time to take a closer look at the wisdom that Pythagoras shared with his followers and that has been handed down to us today.

PHILOSOPHY AND RELIGION

Pythagoras was the first man in history to refer to himself as a philosopher, which literally means "a lover of wisdom." To the Pythagoreans, the distinction between philosophy and religion was blurry. Their teachings regarding the human soul and religion were a combination of mystical beliefs and a more scientific

pursuit of knowledge. Pythagoras was open to knowledge in any form it might take, including the religious traditions of many countries and cultures.

The fundamental principle in Pythagorean thought is the absolute belief in and reverence for numbers. To Pythagoras, numbers were the essence of all human knowledge and existence. It was only through the study of numbers that men and women could hope to understand the workings of the soul, as well as the universe around them. The Pythagoreans used numbers to create a model of the universe. They also used numbers to determine on which days they should worship in the temple. They believed that the world's secrets would be revealed to those who held the key, and that key was numbers.

The Soul

Pythagoras believed that the soul was made of three essential parts: reason, emotion, and intelligence. In Pythagoras's native land of Samos, this three-part conception was the least controversial aspect of his theories regarding the soul. Pythagoras's travels in Egypt and the East had introduced him to concepts regarding the soul that were unfamiliar to the ancient Greeks. The Pythagoreans believed that the human

Ancient Greeks believed that if a dead person received the proper burial rites, his or her soul would be guided to the underworld, known as Hades. Hades was named after the god of the underworld, who was also known as Pluto. The above photo shows the Necromanteion of Ephyra near modern-day Mesopotamo in northwest Greece. This is an ancient sanctuary devoted to Hades and his wife, Persephone.

world in conflict. Pythagoras's followers believed that there was a way to bring the limited into harmony with the unlimited. As usual in Pythagorean thought, the answer lay in mathematics and music. To understand mathematics was to understand music. To understand both was thought to give people the ability to see the invisible workings of the unlimited.

Worship of the Gods

Because the Pythagorean society on Croton was as much a religious community as it was a philosophical or mathematical one, the worship of the gods was central to the Pythagorean way of life. Above all, the Pythagoreans revered the ancient Greek god Apollo, who was the god of the sun, music, art, medicine, prophecy, and philosophy. Given the subjects that the Pythagoreans pursued—mathematics, music, geometry, and philosophy—it is not surprising that Apollo was a central figure of honor.

The Pythagoreans were very particular about the methods that they used for worshipping the gods. The

Apollo, a god particularly revered by Pythagoreans, appears on this one-handled jug from the sixth century BC. The image illustrates one of the myths concerning the half-brothers Hercules and Apollo, sons of Zeus. Hercules is being chased by Apollo after Hercules stole the tripod (a sacred three-legged stool from the Oracle of Delphi).

rituals that they adopted were a combination of ancient Greek and Egyptian religious practices. The Pythagoreans' belief in the sacredness of numbers also seems to have had an effect on their religious practices. The concept of the limited and unlimited played a role

Animal sacrifices were an important part of ancient Greek religious rituals. These offerings were thought to please the gods, purify the worshipper, and bring good fortune. In the above fifth-century-BC carving taken from the Parthenon, some Greek youths lead an ox to sacrifice. Though a vegetarian, Pythagoras was thought to have supported animal sacrifices, believing that human souls would know not to enter any animal destined for ritual sacrifice.

in religious worship, too. Pythagoras adopted key elements from Egyptian religious rituals, such as burning incense and herbs as sacrifices to the gods. Numbers determined the proper days on which to worship. All libations—sacrifices of liquids, such as wine—were made three times to mirror the utterances of the Pythian priestesses of the Oracle of Delphi who spoke their prophecies over tripods (three-legged stools).

Pythagoras urged his followers to enter temples on the right side, which they associated with the unlimited, and exit temples on the left, which they associated with the limited. According to the third-century-AD neo-Pythagorean Iamblichus, entering the temple represents entering the unlimited. Exiting it represents a return to the world of humans, the limited. Pythagoras urged his followers to keep the limited and unlimited separate by not burning the bodies of the dead. As flames were considered sacred, it would be inappropriate to bring this divine, unlimited element into contact with a physical body, the ultimate symbol of the limited.

NUMEROLOGY

Understanding the contributions that Pythagoras made to the science of mathematics and geometry

begins with a look at something altogether less scientific—numerology. Numerology is the study of the supernatural power of numbers and their supposed ability to influence events in people's lives. Pythagoras and his followers believed that numbers were real, not just symbols, and existed independently of anything that they might represent. The Pythagoreans also believed that numbers had personalities and characteristics.

Pythagoreans accepted only whole, positive numbers as actual numbers. In other words, they did not deal with fractions, negative numbers, or even the number 0. They believed that odd numbers represented the unlimited, the world of the Gods, the world that most people cannot see or even comprehend. Odd numbers also symbolized maleness, stillness, the right, and the good. Even numbers, on the other hand, represented the limited, the visible world of humans. For Pythagoras, even numbers also symbolized the female, motion, the left, darkness, and evil. Interestingly, the Pythagoreans considered the number 1 as both odd and even.

Pythagoras attributed very specific characteristics to certain numbers. He considered the first ten numbers as sacred, with 10 being the most sacred of all. Each number was given a name and a set of defining properties.

The number 1, called the monad, was the origin of everything—the starting point of all life and other numbers. The monad was sacred because the Pythagoreans believed that it existed in every number, especially 2 through 10, the other sacred numbers. The monad number represented the divine to the Pythagoreans. It was the symbol of existence and being.

The number 2, called the dyad, represented creation. It embodied duality and opposites. The Pythagoreans considered it a daring number for having the courage to break away from the monad. The dyad could potentially express the conflict that arises from opposites.

The number 3, or the triad, was the first true number. It expressed a multitude, or many, and symbolized wholeness because it contains the beginning, the middle, and the end. To the Pythagoreans, the number 3 represented the soul, which they thought consisted of three parts: reason, emotion, and intelligence. The triad was also considered the symbol of matter, as matter is three-dimensional. Finally, the number 3 exemplified knowledge, a place of honor for the Pythagoreans, and therefore was thought of as the first true number. The Pythagoreans, who revered oracles, pointed out that the tripod used by the Pythian priestess had three legs.

The priestess of Apollo who served at the Oracle of Delphi, known as the Pythia, would sit on a tripod—a three-legged stool—that was placed over a crack in the temple floor. From out of this crack rose fumes that seemed to put the Pythia into a trance. While entranced, the Pythia would answer questions asked by worshippers. Her muttered replies were famous for their lack of clarity and directness. Above is a fifth-century-BC kylix, or drinking cup, bearing the image of Aegeus, a mythical king of Athens, consulting the oracle who sits atop the tripod.

The tetrad was the name given to the number 4. The tetrad represented completion. Four was the number of seasons in the year as well as the number of the four basic elements: earth, air, fire, and water. Four is a number associated with musical intervals, so the tetrad was also sacred in music. Finally, the

tetrad was the number associated with planetary movement, which the Pythagoreans believed created musical sounds.

The number 5, named the pentad, was considered holy because it was the number that exemplified marriage and love. It stood for the coming together of opposites, in particular men and women. The Pythagoreans saw the number 5 as the sum of the first even and odd number, 2 plus 3 (as 1 was neither exclusively odd or even, but both at the same time).

The next number, 6, or the hexad as it was called, represented health to the Pythagoreans. It was the number of balance in the world. The Pythagoreans had a mathematical reason for this. First, the sum of the first three numbers—1, 2, and 3—equals 6. Also, if multiplied, these same three numbers again equal 6. For the Pythagoreans, who considered all things in the world fundamentally mathematical in nature, the fact that the sum and multiplication of the first three numbers would yield the same number was evidence that the gods spoke in numbers. Therefore, the hexad held a place of honor among the sacred numbers.

The number 7, called the heptad, symbolized the human body because the head has seven openings (mouth, two nostrils, two ears, two eyes). Also, the

body has seven basic body parts: the head, the neck, the torso, two legs, and two arms. It expressed, too, the sacred musical instrument, the lyre, which had seven strings. The heptad was considered the fortress of numbers—7 cannot be divided by any number other than itself. Finally, it symbolized the Pythagoreans' seven basic ages of a human: infant, child, adolescent, young adult, adult, elder, and old person.

The octad was the name given to the number 8. It embodied friendship and steadfastness for Pythagoras's followers. It was the first number that was a cube—a number multiplied by itself, with the product again multiplied by that number. For example: 2 x 2 = 4 and 4 x 2 = 8. Eight was a sacred number musically, because it is the basic number of all musical ratios.

The number 9, or the ennead, acted as the horizon or threshold to the most sacred of all numbers, 10. For this reason, the number 9 was also referred to as the Oceanus, as it symbolized crossings and passages. The ennead represented the number of months in a pregnancy. Nine was associated with poetry, music, and dance because there were nine muses in Greek mythology. The muses were goddesses of art and science—astronomy, comedy, dancing, epic poetry, history, lyric poetry, music, sacred poetry, and tragedy. People believed that artists and thinkers

The Greek goddesses who represented the arts and sciences and inspired artists, poets, philosophers, and musicians were known as the muses. Early Greek mythology mentions only one muse. Eventually nine were identified—Calliope, Clio, Erato, Euterpe, Melpomene, Polyhymnia, Terpsichore, Thalia, and Urania. They were said to be the daughters of Zeus and Mnemosyne, the goddess of memory, and sang of the world's creation, and the greatness of Zeus and other gods and heroes. The three Muses shown above in the base of a fourth-century-BC statue watch and judge a music contest between Apollo and Marsyas, a flute-playing shepherd.

were inspired by the nine Muses to do great work in their particular field.

The number 10, which Pythagoras and his followers called the decad, was the most sacred number of all. It was the number of eternity and divinity, and was considered the number that held all of the forces

of the world together. According to Pythagoras, ten was the number of spheres that floated in the heavens. As such, all other numbers circled around this sacred number. Ten was the sum of 1 + 2 + 3 + 4, the four most sacred numbers coming before ten. One of the reasons that the Pythagoreans considered 1, 2, 3, and 4 sacred was because they represented the three basic musical ratios: 4:3, 3:2, and 2:1.

The decad was also embodied in the Pythagoreans' most sacred symbol, the tetractus. In the Pythagorean tradition, the tetractus was not written as we would write the number today. Instead it was noted by a series of dots in a triangular shape (see figure 2, page 71). The tetractus denoted 1 + 2 + 3 + 4 = 10, and was the numerical model of the soul and the universe.

The Pythagoreans' belief in numerology may seem a bit unusual in the twenty-first century, but these mystical beliefs were very much a part of the sixth century BC and were certainly a part of the education that Pythagoras received in Egypt and Babylon. Mysticism is the belief that the spiritual understanding of a subject is more important than what is experienced or observed. Pythagorean numerology was certainly part of a mystical tradition. Due to the mystical elements of Pythagoras's teaching, some

historians have been ready to discredit him as a quack with little to offer in terms of real mathematics. Perhaps it would be more appropriate to see these numerological beliefs as the result of Pythagoras's passion for numbers, a passion that some say was the very start of mathematics as we know it today.

MATHEMATICS AND GEOMETRY

To the Pythagoreans, there was only one hope for understanding the world; that hope was mathematics. Numerology may have played a large role in their attempt to piece together how the world works, but rigorous scientific methods also played an important role. Philolaus, a Pythagorean who lived about 100 years after Pythagoras, brought some of Pythagoras's mathematical theories to the forefront. The Pythagoreans' study of numbers yielded some of the first genuine mathematical and geometrical theories in Western thought.

The way in which Pythagoras and his followers conceived of numbers was very different from the way mathematics is practiced today. In addition to representing quantities, numbers symbolized geometrical shapes. Therefore, the Pythagoreans'

study of geometry was linked closely to the study of mathematics. Today, numbers are portrayed by symbols. The concept of the number two, for instance, is written as the numeral 2. Pythagoreans used a much more ancient form of writing to represent numbers. Pythagorean mathematicians represented numbers by a series of equidistant (equally spaced) dots that formed lines, triangles, rectangles, and so forth (see figure 1). These numbers look very much like the markings found on dice or dominoes. In this way, Pythagoreans were able to see and change the shape of every number.

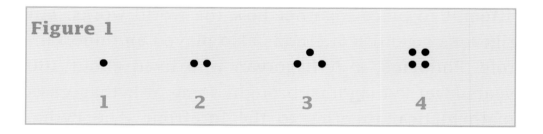

Figure 1

1   2   3   4

The Pythagoreans placed their most important numbers into four basic categories: triangles, squares, rectangles, and gnomons. Triangular numbers include any number that can be shaped into a triangle, using a series of dots. The numbers 3 and 10 (see figure 2) are examples of triangular numbers.

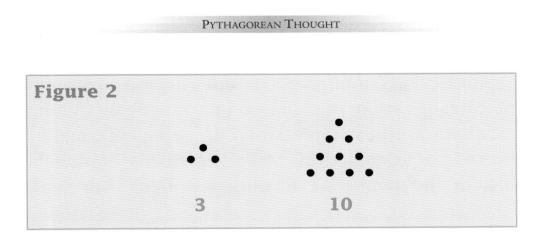

Figure 2

3

10

Square numbers are those that can be shaped into a square. Examples include the numbers 4 and 9 (see figure 3).

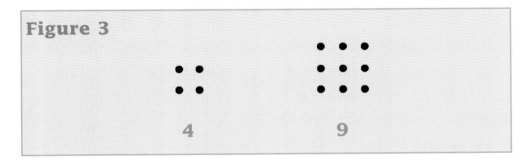

Figure 3

4

9

Take a closer look at the numbers 4 and 9. Their dots form squares, and these numbers are, indeed, what today we call square numbers. Four is the square of 2 (the product of a number multiplied by itself; 2 x 2 = 4), just as 9 is the square of 3 (3 x 3 = 9). The Pythagoreans did not just call these numbers squares; they actually visualized and wrote them as squares. Their system of representation using dots made the geometric properties of numbers easier to understand.

The next set of numbers in the Pythagorean system of categorization was the oblong numbers. Oblong numbers are best understood as being rectangular in shape. Examples of these rectangular numbers include the numbers 2, 6, and 8 (see figure 4).

Figure 4

2   6   8

Finally there is the group called the gnomons. Gnomon was the name of the sundial of Babylonian origin first used in Greece by Anaximander, Pythagoras's teacher in Miletus. The origin of the word "gnomon" may relate to the L-shaped indicator on a sundial that casts a shadow and indicates the approximate time of day. The gnomons are odd numbers and are represented by the shape of a carpenter's square (an L shape).

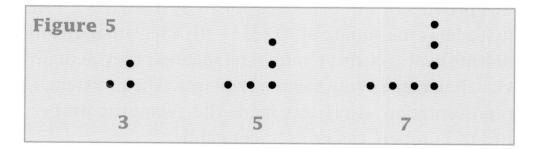

Figure 5

3   5   7

This method of representing and categorizing numbers is often seen as the very beginning of modern mathematics. Using this system, the Pythagoreans were able to manipulate numbers in a variety of ways. For example, they proposed that any two successive triangular numbers make a square number, and then demonstrated the theory using their system of numerical representation. As shown in figure 6 below, when two consecutive triangular numbers, such as 3 and 6, are added together, they make a square number, 9.

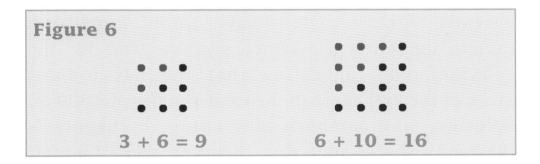

Figure 6

$3 + 6 = 9$ $6 + 10 = 16$

THE PYTHAGOREAN THEOREM

All of this tinkering with numbers and their shapes was bound to result in at least a few groundbreaking mathematical theories. Today most people associate Pythagoras with a single mathematical theorem that now bears his name—the Pythagorean theorem. The

Pythagorean theorem states that in a right triangle—a triangle that has a 90-degree angle—the sum of the squares of the lengths of the two shorter sides equals the square of the length of the longest side. No student escapes an introduction to geometry course without learning that Pythagoras was the first to pronounce officially that $a^2 + b^2 = c^2$. But was Pythagoras truly the originator of this theorem?

Today, historians know that Pythagoras and his followers were not the first to make use of this theorem. There is some evidence that the Egyptians made use of it for many centuries before the Pythagoreans. Archaeologists have found cuneiform tablets (an ancient writing system used by the Babylonians), suggesting that the Babylonians knew of the Pythagorean theorem as early as 1800 BC. Milesian philosophers, including Pythagoras's teachers, Thales and Anaximander, were familiar with Babylonian science. Some historians believe that Pythagoras learned about the theorem while studying with these men. Scientists have also found evidence that the people of India and China knew about the theorem as far back as 500 BC. One modern historian has even suggested that the theorem should be named the pre-Pythagorean theorem.

Does this mean that Pythagoras should not take credit for the theorem $a^2 + b^2 = c^2$? A closer look at the work that the Pythagoreans did with this theorem brings to light why it has become so closely associated with them. Pythagoras and his followers may not have been the first to make use of the theorem, but they were the first to attempt to explain it scientifically.

A right triangle is one in which two of the triangle's sides are perpendicular to each other, forming a right, or 90-degree, angle. The Pythagorean theorem states that with a right triangle, the sum of the squares of the lengths of the two shorter sides of the triangle equals the square of the length of the longest side. The hypotenuse, or the longest side, gets its name from the two Greek words, *hypo*, meaning "below," and *tenuse*, meaning "stretch." The longest line in a right triangle is the line that stretches opposite the right angle.

Today's mathematical methods lead us to think of the Pythagorean theorem in strictly numerical terms. When we say $a^2 + b^2 = c^2$, we imagine multiplying *a* by *a* and adding that to *b* multiplied by *b*. This sum would be the same number as *c* multiplied by *c*. The Pythagoreans would be more likely to explain the theorem in the following way: the square built on the hypotenuse is equal to the sum of the

squares built on the two shorter sides of the right triangle. The diagram below shows what the Pythagoreans meant by building the square on the lines of the triangle.

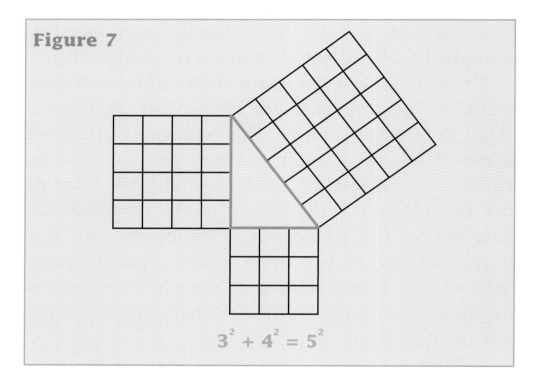

Figure 7

$$3^2 + 4^2 = 5^2$$

PYTHAGORAS'S IMPORTANCE TO THE DEVELOPMENT OF MATHEMATICS

In addition to the Pythagorean theorem, Pythagoras is credited with six other mathematical theorems. One of these is the theorem that states that eight triangular

numbers (made up of the same number of dots) plus 1 equals a square number. As the diagram below shows, this theorem could also be demonstrated visually.

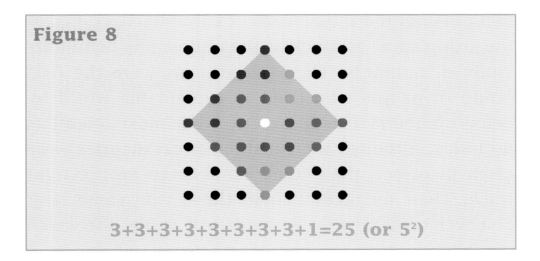

Figure 8

3+3+3+3+3+3+3+3+1=25 (or 5^2)

Eight triangular numbers (of the same number of dots) plus 1 equals a square number.

It is difficult to say whether the mathematical work associated with the Pythagoreans was Pythagoras's own or the work of his disciples, or a collaborative effort between master and pupils. The Pythagorean community's secrecy has made it difficult to answer this question. Pythagoras may not have been personally responsible for discovering all of the mathematical theories attributed to him, but he was certainly the inspiration that led to this innovative

exploration of numbers and provided the physical and intellectual setting in which important discoveries could be made.

The most important aspect of Pythagorean mathematics is not the actual mathematical discoveries that the group made as much as the philosophy behind its study of numbers. The Pythagoreans were the first group of people who tried to explain the world by using numbers. This is exactly what most scientists do today. Although their mathematical theories were often incorrect, the Pythagoreans were on the right track. Their mistakes helped those who came later discover some of the mathematical truths for which the Pythagoreans had been searching.

Other philosophers of the time considered the Pythagoreans' emphasis on numbers to be a little ridiculous. The ancient Greek world was just beginning its scientific journey. Perhaps the Pythagoreans were a little ahead of their time when it came to numbers. Their reverence for numbers may at times have been mystical and unscientific, but it did begin an exploration that laid the groundwork for future generations of mathematicians, not to mention astronomers, geographers, engineers, and other scientists who would remake the world and our understanding of it.

COSMOLOGY AND ASTRONOMY

One of the key areas of study for the Pythagoreans was heavenly bodies. As with every other subject that they investigated, their ideas regarding the heavens were a mix of religious beliefs and hard science. Cosmology is the study of the origin and nature of the universe. It is a subject that tends to be speculative (involving mystical beliefs rather than direct, empirical observation). Astronomy, on the other hand, is the more scientific attempt to study the behavior of matter in outer space. Pythagoras's theories and observations about Earth, the sun, and planets were a combination of these two fields. As with much of Pythagorean mathematics, much of what we know about the group's cosmological and astronomical work comes from Philolaus.

The Pythagoreans believed they had achieved a complete understanding of the creation and structure of the universe. According to Pythagoras's conception, the universe was made of ten spheres. These ten spheres were the sun, moon, Earth, the five additional known planets at the time—Mercury, Venus, Mars, Jupiter, and Saturn—the counter-Earth, and the central hearth. Two of these bodies, the counter-Earth and the central hearth, were not observable in space.

According to Pythagorean cosmology, the central hearth lay at the very center of the universe and was the origin of all of the other spheres. It was referred to as "the guard post of Zeus." Zeus was the father and leader of the twelve Olympian Greek gods (the twelve major gods of ancient Greek religion, named after Mount Olympus, where Zeus ruled with his wife, Hera). The Pythagoreans believed that the central hearth was the starting point of the universe and that it provided life and light to the world. Earth rotated around the hearth.

This Roman statue of Jupiter from the third century AD is based on a Greek original of Zeus. Like Zeus, who was adapted by the Romans, Jupiter was the most powerful of the Roman gods. Also like Zeus, Jupiter was the god of the sky, as well as of rain, thunder, and lightning. Both Jupiter and Zeus are usually depicted as large, muscular, bearded men carrying a thunderbolt in one hand (as shown at left). Because it is the largest and second-brightest planet in our solar system (behind Venus), the Romans named the planet after the king of gods, Jupiter.

Whether Earth was facing the hearth or not determined day or night.

The counter-Earth was a planetary sphere that, according to the Pythagoreans, was never visible from Earth because it lay on the other side of the central hearth. Aristotle accused the Pythagoreans of making up the counter-Earth simply so that there would be ten heavenly bodies instead of nine and, therefore, fit neatly into their numerological system. The number 10 was sacred to the Pythagoreans, and the idea of ten heavenly bodies may have been so irresistible to Pythagoras that he simply created a fictional sphere to reach that number.

Music and numbers were central to the Pythagoreans' cosmology. Pythagoras believed that the planets, the sun, and the moon all moved around the central hearth according to musical ratios. They believed that this planetary movement created musical sounds. Although most men and women could not hear this music, Pythagoras claimed that he could. The Pythagoreans believed that the faster a planet moved, the higher the pitch it made while in orbit around the central hearth. The slower-moving planets created lower-pitched music. Historians credit Pythagoras with being the first person to use the word *kosmos* to refer to the universe. *Kosmos* was a

Greek word meaning "harmony." He used this word, which is the root of our words "cosmos" and "cosmology," because he believed that all things in the world, the heavenly bodies in particular, move harmoniously with one another.

As with their mathematics, the Pythagoreans' cosmology and astronomy were a mix of science and religious beliefs. While the central hearth and counter-Earth, along with the music of the planets, may have been mystical constructions on the part of Pythagoras, there are aspects of Pythagorean astronomy that demonstrate a more scientific approach to the study of the heavens.

The Pythagoreans were the first to claim that Earth was not the center of the universe. They believed, instead, that it rotated around a central point, the central hearth. Although they were mistaken about the central point (it is actually the sun), the notion that Earth behaved similarly to other planets in revolving around a central point was revolutionary. In addition, the Pythagoreans believed Earth to be round and suspended in space. During the sixth century BC, most people believed that the world was flat or that it floated on a vast sea. This new idea was a clear departure from traditional thinking. Pythagoras's astronomical theories extended even to the scientific

observation of the morning and evening star. He is credited as the first person to realize that these two stars were the same body. The morning and evening stars are, in fact, the planet Venus.

MUSIC

The Pythagoreans made substantial contributions to the field of musical theory. As was typical of Pythagoras and his followers, their examination of the structure and nature of music combined religious and mystical beliefs with more scientific approaches.

For the Pythagoreans, music was a key element in both everyday and spiritual life. They believed that music had the power to heal a number of physical and mental ailments. They thought that good health depended on the selection of appropriate music. Pythagoras claimed that string instruments had healing powers, but that under no circumstances were his followers to use wind instruments for this purpose. Pythagoras found the sound of wind instruments to be unhelpful and even aggravating to the soul. The Pythagoreans prescribed specific tunes and dances to cure conditions such as rage, anger, and sadness. Pythagoras even asked his followers to listen to specific songs in the morning to help them wake up and

In Greek legend, Orpheus was the symbol of music and thought to be the inventor of the lyre, a harplike stringed instrument. The music he played on the lyre and the songs he sang were said to tame wild animals and alter the normal processes of nature. When his wife, Eurydice, died of a snake bite, Orpheus was overcome with sorrow. The music he played became so sad that even the gods were moved to tears. Orpheus was so devastated that he never loved another woman again. The above 1896 painting by Alexandre Seon, entitled *The Lamentation of Orpheus*, shows Orpheus clutching his lyre, consumed by his grief for Eurydice.

start the day off well. He prescribed a different type of music for falling asleep at night.

Music was also central to the Pythagoreans' religious practices. They worshipped Apollo, the god of music, and were dedicated to Orpheus, the Homeric-age poet who set poetry to music. They integrated

Soothing the Savage Beast

The Pythagoreans were convinced of the power of music. One Pythagorean legend tells how music played a crucial role in a military battle. Croton's neighboring city-state Sybaris had a very powerful cavalry numbering 5,000, which was preparing to attack Croton. The horses of this strong cavalry were trained to parade to music. The Crotonians called on Pythagoras for help. Pythagoras and his disciples played tunes that mesmerized the horses into dancing rather than attacking. With Sybaris's cavalry prancing and high-stepping rather than charging, Croton was able to win the battle.

A group of horses surges in unison in this fifth-century-BC sculpture relief from the Lycian sarcophagus, housed in the Archaeological Museum in Istanbul, Turkey. This is a detail from a scene of a lion hunt carved on the side of the sarcophagus (a stone coffin). The other side features a boar hunt.

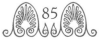

music, poetry, and dance into their religious ceremonies. Unfortunately, none of the Pythagorean tunes survived, so the sound of their music has been lost to the ages.

MUSIC AND MATHEMATICS

For Pythagoras and his followers, music and mathematics were inseparable. It was the combination of these two elements that allowed people to understand the unlimited concept of the universe. The Pythagoreans thought music was the manifestation of

Pythagoras conducts sound experiments in this fifteenth-century woodcut from Venice, Italy. Supposedly inspired by the sound of blacksmiths' hammers and their varying tones, Pythagoras began a series of experiments using bells, water glasses, strings, and flutes that were designed to discover the mathematical ratios behind the most pleasing musical harmonies. Pythagoras is shown striking the bells labeled 8 and 16. In this way, he is shown to be discovering the octave.

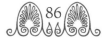

harmony in the world. They believed that for those who possessed a certain kind of knowledge, the musical harmony of the world could be heard, especially in the movement of the planets.

But what did Pythagoras mean when he said that music and mathematics were closely related to one another? The answer to this question is well illustrated by the story of Pythagoras's discovery of musical ratios. According to tradition, Pythagoras was strolling by a blacksmith's shop when he realized that the sound of pounding hammers was creating a musical sound. Curious, he went into the shop and inquired about the hammers the blacksmith used. As the story goes, the hammers' weight ratios were six, eight, nine, and twelve. Upon learning this, Pythagoras returned to his community and began experimenting with an instrument called a monochord (so named because it only has one string). By dividing the one string on the monochord at different places and then plucking it, the Pythagoreans were able to begin their experiments with musical ratios.

According to Pythagoras, the ratios of the blacksmith's weights when applied to the monochord's string created the same musical consonance that he had heard coming from the blacksmith's pounding hammers. A musical consonance is a combination of

sounds that occur at the same time that many people consider harmonious and pleasing to the human ear. When sounded simultaneously, Pythagoras's humming strings demonstrated that certain ratios created pleasing sounds. Using the humming string of the monochord, Pythagoras was able to name three musical ratios that musicians continue to use today. They are the ratio 2:1, which represents a musical octave; 3:2, which represents a musical fifth; and 4:3, which represents a musical fourth. How do these ratios correspond to the blacksmith's hammers? The hammers weighed 6, 8, 9, and 12 pounds (2.7, 3.6, 4.1, 5.4 kilograms). When the ratio 12:6 is simplified, it becomes 2:1. Similarly, 9:6 is the same as 3:2, and 8:6 is 4:3. To the spiritually minded Pythagoreans, the fact that the three musical ratios that they discovered included only the sacred numbers 1, 2, 3, and 4 was nothing short of miraculous. In addition, these four numbers added up to 10, the mystical tetractus. They considered it just one more indication that the world was arranged according to numbers.

Since Pythagoras's lifetime, many more musical ratios have been discovered, but the Pythagoreans were the first to make the direct connection between music and numbers. Given their groundbreaking

work with music, it is not surprising that the work of Pythagoras and his followers is considered the foundation upon which all Western music theory is based. As with numbers, the Pythagoreans' religious beliefs and practices resulted in discoveries that were as much a part of the realm of science as they were of faith.

7 PYTHAGORAS'S LEGACY

Unfortunately for Pythagoras and his followers, the society they had created in Croton did not last for more than a few decades. Political events in Croton ensured that the community's end was as sudden as it was brutal. The stable and prosperous colony that Pythagoras had chosen for his school had grown in power and wealth, but not all of its citizens were happy with its government. They were particularly angry at the strong influence that the Pythagoreans had on the ruling class that held most of the power in Croton.

During the school's existence, the Pythagoreans' sway over the colony's government had steadily grown. The rulers of Croton were a small group of aristocrats, many of whom were followers of Pythagoras. As political instability grew in Croton, so did the average Crotonians' resentment

Pythagoras studies by candlelight in this mid-eighteenth-century oil painting by Pietro Longhi, a history, religious, and portrait painter from Venice, Italy. Pythagoras is depicted in a manner similar to that of Christian hermits and saints who retire from the world to live alone in poverty and devote themselves to study and meditation.

of Pythagoras's influence on their government. The people's distrust of the Pythagorean community was in part due to the school's secretiveness. Here was a group that did not reveal any of its teachings yet played a major political role in people's lives.

PYTHAGORAS'S EXILE AND DEATH

People opposed to Pythagoras's political influence decided it was time to rid Croton of the philosopher and his followers. They called a people's assembly where they decided that the aristocrats, and the Pythagoreans in particular, must be expelled from Croton. Their methods were violent and effective. During a

An 1887 oil painting by Michele Tedesco entitled *A Pythagorean School Invaded by Sybarites* depicts the austere and serious Pythagorean students being overrun and harassed by the luxury-loving, wealthy citizens of Sybaris, a neighboring town that was avenging Croton's attack upon it in 510 BC.

large indoor meeting of the Pythagorean community, the opponents burned down the building in which the group had gathered. Pythagoras was one of the few who survived. After the slaughter in Croton, Pythagoras retired from public life. However, the persecution of the Pythagoreans did not stop. They were chased throughout southern Italy. Even non-members who sympathized with them were persecuted and killed.

For Pythagoras, sadly, the end was very near. He was almost 100 years old. The details of Pythagoras's death are not clear. Some historians believe that he spent some time moving from one southern Italian

colony to another, trying to stay one step ahead of those who wanted to kill him. According to tradition, Pythagoras sought refuge in the Temple of the Muses in the southern Italian colony of Metapontum. His attackers did not dare to go into such a sacred place to kill him, but neither did they allow any of his supporters to enter in order to assist him. Many believe that Pythagoras, cut off from outside supplies, eventually died of starvation in the temple.

After Pythagoras's death, his followers spread out from Italy into Sicily and Greece. A generation later, some of the Pythagoreans returned to Croton and reestablished the school that their master had founded. The new school in Croton lasted until about 300 BC. Aristaeus, a close disciple of Pythagoras's, took over as the society's leader and even married Pythagoras's widow. After Aristaeus, Pythagoras's eldest son, Mnesarchus, took over the school. However, the society's influence would never again regain the stature, respect, and fame it enjoyed under Pythagoras.

PYTHAGORAS'S INFLUENCE SPREADS AND ENDURES

Before Pythagoras died, many philosophers and mathematicians knew of his ideas. But after his death

and the destruction of his society, Pythagoras's ideas spread even wider and faster. Some saw the Pythagoreans as an extreme group of religious fanatics and attempted to discredit them and their teachings. Others looked past their strange, secretive way of life to discover the practical value of their theories regarding numbers, music, and astronomy.

Plato is perhaps the best known and most respected name in ancient Greek philosophy. One of Plato's mentors was a Pythagorean from Sicily named Archytas. Considered the first master mathematician in the Pythagorean tradition, Archytas's influence on Plato is unmistakable. In Plato's most scientific work, *Timaeus*, he claims that musical ratios guide heavenly bodies, a belief traced directly back to Pythagoras. Additionally, Plato's belief in a visible and an invisible world mirrors Pythagoras's conception of limited and unlimited worlds.

By the second century AD, all of the Pythagorean societies had vanished. The Roman philosophers, however, revived Pythagorean thought. They closely associated Pythagorean thought with Plato's ideas, which were also in the midst of a revival. During this period, the neo-Platonic and neo-Pythagorean traditions became blended, so much so that it is difficult to tell one from the other.

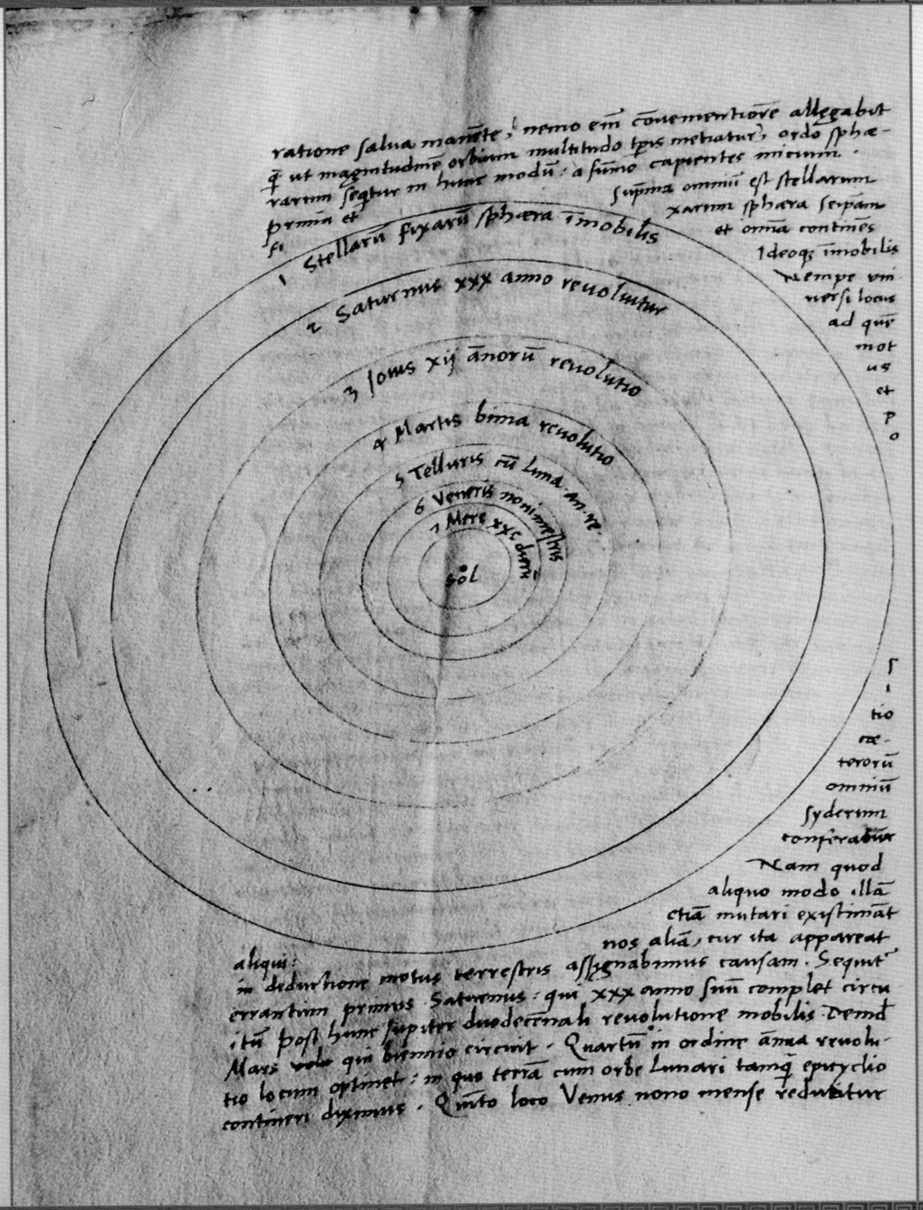

A manuscript page from Polish astronomer Nicolaus Copernicus's treatise *De Revolutionibus Orbium Coelestium Libri Sex* (About the Revolutions of the Heavenly Spheres in Six Books) appears above. The book first appeared in 1543, and Copernicus died soon after its publication. In this book, Copernicus made the then-revolutionary claim that the sun—and not Earth—was the center of the universe. Copernicus credited Pythagoras with providing the foundation for his groundbreaking studies.

Many centuries later, Pythagoras's influence continued. In 1530, Polish-born Nicolaus Copernicus (1473–1543), the first modern astronomer, claimed that the sun was at the center of our universe and that Earth rotated around the sun. In making this claim, Copernicus contradicted the prevailing view at the time that Earth was the center of the universe around which everything else revolved. To escape punishment from religious authorities who insisted that God had made Earth and man the center of the universe, Copernicus did not publish his findings until soon before his death. Today, the

Like Pythagoras, who greatly influenced him, early seventeenth-century astronomer Johannes Kepler believed that the universe was created by a divine being according to mathematical principles. Though as a student he was taught that Earth was the center of the universe, he supported the Copernican idea (itself strongly influenced by Pythagoras) of six planets revolving around the sun in perfectly circular orbits. Kepler eventually realized that planetary orbits were elliptical, or oval-shaped.

Copernican system is widely accepted. In his writings, Copernicus expresses gratitude to Pythagoras for laying the groundwork for his astronomical discovery.

German astronomer Johannes Kepler (1571–1630) credited Pythagoras as the inspiration for his many discoveries in mathematics and astronomy. During the sixteenth century, Kepler proved that Copernicus had been correct—Kepler's laws of planetary motion show the sun to be the center of the universe. Kepler even went so far as to call himself a Pythagorean, because he, like Pythagoras, believed that a divine being created the universe according to mathematical principles.

Today, Pythagoras is remembered primarily as a mathematician. However, his influence also extends to current religious beliefs and music theory. The ideas he formulated concerning the soul's immortality and transmigration influenced thinkers from Plato to modern-day spiritualists. Pythagoras's work in music theory led Sir Isaac Newton (1642–1727), the famous Enlightenment scientist and philosopher, to credit him with discovering musical ratios.

Despite Pythagoras's influential legacy in a variety of fields, he remains a mysterious, poorly understood figure. Today's scholars are still debating whether Pythagoras was one of the very first true scientists or

Pythagoras's pioneering astronomical studies had a profound impact on later astronomers, whose discoveries made space travel possible in the second half of the twentieth century. The National Aeronautics and Space Administration (NASA) acknowledged the debt owed to the pioneering thinkers of the ancient world by naming its first three manned space programs after figures from classical mythology. In this photograph, *Apollo 11*—the mission that first put men on the moon—is launched on July 16, 1969.

simply a religious fanatic who happened to have some insight into mathematics and music and made a few lucky guesses about the nature of the universe. Scholars question whether Pythagoras is even responsible for the ideas and discoveries attributed to him. Given the scarcity of primary sources, historians may never answer these questions satisfactorily. Perhaps they do not need to be answered.

The clear distinction drawn between science and faith during the twenty-first century might have appeared strange and unnatural to Pythagoras, who saw no contradiction or seam between the two. His faith in numbers and their harmonious ordering of the universe led Pythagoras to investigations that changed the way future generations perceived the world.

Today, mathematics underlies and drives our inventions and discoveries in fields ranging from astronomy and computer science to medicine and music. The modern world is built upon a foundation of numbers. Skyscrapers, bridges, superhighways, mass media, telecommunications systems, computer culture, and Internet technology—none of these achievements would have been possible without an understanding of numbers and their practical uses. We have Pythagoras to thank for introducing us to the awe-inspiring power of numbers.

TIMELINE

circa 560 BC	Pythagoras is born on the island of Samos. His father is Mnesarchus of Tyre, a merchant. His mother is Parthenis, a Samos native. In his youth he was taught by the philosopher Pherecydes on the island of Syros.

circa 560 BC	Pythagoras travels to Miletus and studies under the famous and respected philosophers Thales and Thales' pupil, Anaximander. In Miletus, Pythagoras was probably instructed in mathematics, astronomy, geometry, and cosmology.

circa 535 BC	Following the advice of Thales, Pythagoras journeys to Egypt and becomes influenced by Egyptian spiritual traditions and practices and is eventually accepted into the priesthood.

525 BC	Cambyses II, king of Persia, invades Egypt. Pythagoras is taken prisoner and exiled to Babylon, where he studies under Persian magi and learns their sacred rites and mystical traditions. He also studies math and music there.

circa 520 BC	Pythagoras gains his freedom and leaves Babylon, eventually returning to Samos and founding his school, the Semicircle.

circa 518 BC	Pythagoras leaves Samos and travels to southern Italy, where he eventually founds a religious and philosophical society at Croton.
circa 508 BC	The Pythagorean society at Croton is attacked by Cylon, a wealthy nobleman of Croton who had been refused membership in the society due to his violent tendencies and unpleasant personality. Pythagoras escapes to Metapontium, where he is said to have died. Some accounts suggest he killed himself in despair over the destruction of his society in Croton. A related account reports that he sought refuge in Metapontium's Temple of the Muses and starved to death there. Others accounts claim that Pythagoras failed to escape Croton but was killed by Cylon's men. One tradition insists that he actually returned to Croton and lived to be about 100 years old.
500 BC	The Pythagorean society thrives and expands, spreading to other Italian cities.
circa 460 BC	After becoming more and more political in nature and splitting into several factions, meeting houses of the Pythagorean society throughout Italy, including in Croton, are attacked and burned. The society itself is suppressed and outlawed.

GLOSSARY

Apollo Ancient Greek god of the sun, music, and prophecy; one of the twelve gods of Olympus.

communal Characterized by shared ownership and use of property or shared experiences and responsibilities in a domestic setting.

cosmology The study of the origin, history, and dynamics of the universe.

cuneiform Wedge-shaped characters used in ancient Sumerian, Assyrian, Babylonian, and Persian writing.

exile A period of forced or voluntary absence from one's country or home.

hypotenuse The side of a right triangle opposite the right angle.

infinite Endless, without limit, eternal.

initiation The rites and ceremonies by which one is made a member of a club or society.

Ionian A member of any of the Greek people who settled on the islands of the Aegean Sea and the western shore of Asia Minor toward the end of the second millennium BC.

lyre A stringed instrument of the harp family that has two curved arms connected at the upper end by a crossbar, used primarily in ancient Greece.

magi Babylonian wise men of Persia's priest class.

Muses The nine daughters of Mnemosyne and Zeus, each of whom presided over a different art or science. They were considered the source of artistic inspiration.

numerology The study of the supposed hidden influence of numbers on human affairs.

oracle A person (usually a priest or priestess in ancient times) through whom the gods are thought to speak; or the shrine where a deity reveals hidden wisdom through a person.

oral tradition The spoken relation and preservation, from one generation to the next, of cultural history and ancestry.

papyrus A writing material made from the pith or the stems of the papyrus plant; used especially by the ancient Egyptians, Greeks, and Romans.

Pythian priestesses Priestesses who served at the Oracle of Delphi and, under the influence of divine inspiration, answered the questions of those who came to honor the god Apollo.

temporal Relating to time (as opposed to eternity) and earthly life.

FOR MORE INFORMATION

American Mathematical Society
201 Charles Street
Providence, RI 02904-2294
(800) 321-4AMS (4267)
Web site: http://www.ams.org

American Philosophical Society
104 South Fifth Street
Philadelphia, PA 19106-3387
(215) 440-3400 (4267)
Web site: http://www.amphilsoc.org

American School of Classical Studies in Athens
54 Souedias Street
GR-106 76 Athens
Greece
3 (021) 0723-6313
Web site: http://www.ascsa.edu.gr

Institute for Byzantine and Modern Greek Studies, Inc.
115 Gilbert Road
Belmont, MA 02178-2200
(617) 484-6595
Web site: http://www.orthodoxinfo.com/ibmgs

WEB SITES

Due to the changing nature of Internet links, the
Rosen Publishing Group, Inc., has developed an
online list of Web sites related to the subject of
this book. This site is updated regularly. Please
use this link to access the list:

http://www.rosenlinks.com/lgp/pyth

FOR FURTHER READING

Baker, Rosalie F., and Charles F. Baker III. *Ancient Greeks: Creating the Classical Tradition*. New York, NY: Oxford University Press, 1997.

Courant, Richard, and Herbert Robbins; revised by Ian Stewart. *What Is Mathematics?: An Elementary Approach to Ideas and Methods*. New York, NY: Oxford University Press, 1996.

Gay, Kathlyn. *Science in Ancient Greece*. New York, NY: Franklin Watts, 1998.

Kahn, Charles H. *Pythagoras and the Pythagoreans: A Brief History*. Indianapolis, IN: Hackett Publishing Company, Inc., 2001.

Nardo, Don. *Scientists of Ancient Greece*. San Diego, CA: Lucent Books, 1999.

Pearson, Anne. *Ancient Greece*. New York, NY: DK Children, 2004.

Shearer, Cynthia A. *The Greenleaf Guide to Famous Men of Greece*. Lebanon, TN: Greenleaf Press, 1989.

Shuler, Jane. *Discoveries, Inventions, and Ideas (The Ancient Greeks)*. Des Plaines, IL: Heinemann Library, 1999.

BIBLIOGRAPHY

Brunschwig, Jaques, and Geoffrey E. R. Lloyd, eds. *A Guide to Greek Thought: Major Figures and Trends.* Cambridge, MA: Belknap Press of Harvard University Press, 2003.

Ellis, Julie. *What's Your Angle, Pythagoras?* Watertown, MA: Charlesbridge Publishing, 2004.

Godwin, Joscelyn. *The Harmony of the Spheres: A Sourcebook of the Pythagorean Tradition in Music.* Rochester, VT: Inner Traditions International, 1993.

Guthrie, Kenneth Sylvan. *The Pythagorean Sourcebook and Library: An Anthology of Ancient Writings Which Relate to Pythagoras and Pythagorean Philosophy.* Grand Rapids, MI: Phanes Press, 1987.

Kahn, Charles H. *Pythagoras and the Pythagoreans: A Brief History.* Indianapolis, IN: Hackett Publishing Company, Inc., 2001.

Mankiewicz, Richard. *The Story of Mathematics.* Princeton, NJ: Princeton University Press, 2000.

Strohmeier, John, and Peter Westbrook. *Divine Harmony: The Life and Teachings of Pythagoras.* Berkeley, CA: Berkeley Hill Books, 1999.

Taylor, Thomas, translator. *Iamblichus' Life of Pythagoras*. Rochester, VT: Inner Traditions International, 1986.

Valens, Evans G. *The Number of Things: Pythagoras, Geometry, and Humming Strings*. New York, NY: Dutton, 1964.

INDEX

A

agriculture, 18, 23, 37
akousmatikoi, 43, 50
Alexander the Great, 6
Anaximander, 17, 20–21, 72, 74
Anaximanes, 17
Apollo, 13, 42, 59, 84
Archytas, 94
Aristaeus, 93
Aristotle, 6, 81
astrology, 28, 29–31
astronomer/astronomy, 18, 22–23, 26, 29, 31, 54, 78, 79–83, 94, 96, 99

B

Babylon/Babylonians, 8, 22–23, 26–31, 32, 74

C

calendar, 29
central hearth, 79–81, 82
Copernicus, Nicolaus, 96–97
cosmology, 18, 21, 54, 79–83

counter-Earth, 79, 81, 82
Croton, 36, 37–40, 45, 50, 53, 59, 85, 90–93
  school at, 40–52, 90–91, 93
cuneiform, 29, 74

D

Damo, 52
diet, 7, 21, 34, 48, 50, 51

E

Egypt/Egyptian, 8, 21, 22–26, 27–29, 31, 34, 41, 46, 55, 74
empiricism, 18

G

geographers/geography, 18, 25, 78
Greece
  Classical period, 6
  scientific age, 22

H

Hades, 56

I

Iamblichus, 48, 61
Ionian school, 8, 15–18, 19, 21

K

Kepler, Johannes, 97

L

limited and unlimited,
    57–58, 60–61, 62, 94

M

mathematics
  Babylonians and, 8, 22–23,
      28–31, 74
  Egyptians and, 8, 22–26,
      28–29, 74
  geometry, 8, 19–20,
      22–23, 25, 54, 59,
      61–62, 69–73, 74
  number system, 29
  philosophy and, 14, 78
mathematikoi, 42–43, 45, 50
Miletus, 15, 17, 19, 20–21, 34
miracles, 42
Mnesarchus (father), 9–12
Mnesarchus (son), 52, 93
Muses, 66–67
music, 7, 12, 28, 85, 94,
    97, 99
  cosmology and, 81, 82,
      86–87
  geometry and, 54
  health and, 83–84
  mathematics and, 58, 86–89

musical ratios, 87, 88,
    94, 97
religion and, 59, 64–65, 66,
    83–86

N

Newton, Isaac, 97
Nile River, 25
numbers
  gnomon, 72
  rectangular, 72
  representation of, 68, 69–73
  reverence for, 55, 60–61,
      61–69, 78, 81, 88–89, 99
  square, 71, 73
  triangular, 70, 73, 76–77
numerology, 61–69, 81

O

Olympic athletes, 37
oracle(s), 61, 63
Orpheus, 84

P

Parthenis (mother), 9
Pherecydes, 12–14
Philolaus, 69, 79
Plato, 6, 19, 22, 94, 97
Pre-Socratics, 6
Pythagoras
  birth, 7, 9
  death, 7, 91–94
  discredited, 69, 78, 94
  education of, 11–14
  as Egyptian priest, 26

family of, 9–12, 52
importance of, 7–8, 76–78, 82–83, 88–89, 93–99
lifestyle, 34, 48–52
myths/legends about, 42, 84
political influence of, 36, 40, 90–91
secrecy of, 33, 40–42, 43, 53, 77, 91, 94
subjects studied by, 7–8, 12, 21, 28, 31
Pythagorean mathematics, 54, 69–78
  origins of, 74, 77, 99
Pythagorean theorem, 7, 73–76
  used before Pythagoras, 22, 29, 74

R
reincarnation, 13, 56
religion/gods, 7–8, 45, 48, 52, 59–61, 89
  Babylonian, 28, 31
  Egyptian, 25–26, 31, 60, 61

mathematics and, 14, 34–35, 54, 65
music and, 83–86
philosophy and, 13–14, 18, 21, 25, 54–55
soul, 13, 26, 45, 50, 54, 55–57, 63, 83, 97

S
Samos, 7, 9, 11, 15, 32–33, 34, 35–36, 37, 55
Semicircle, 32–34
silence, vow of, 46–47
Socrates, 6
Solon, 22
soul, 55–57, 63, 83
students, failed, 47

T
Telauges, 52
Temple of Apollo, 13
Thales, 15–17, 18, 19–21, 22, 74
Theano, 52

ABOUT THE AUTHOR

Dimitra Karamanides earned her master's degree in European history and has been an ancient Greek history and philosophy enthusiast since her early teens. She has lived, worked, and traveled extensively in Greece, including visits to relatives in Miletus—the hometown of Thales, Pythagoras's teacher and mentor, and the birthplace of materialism and modern scientific thought. She has also visited several of the ancient oracles, including Delphi and Dodoni. Today, she lives in New Mexico with her husband, Chris, and two sons, Alexandros and Petros.

PHOTO CREDITS

Cover, pp. 3, 35 Tretyakov Gallery, Moscow, Russia/Bridgeman Art Library; Cover (inset), pp. 3 (inset), 8 Pinacoteca Capitolina, Palazzo Conservatori, Rome/Bridgeman Art Library; p. 7 © Vanni Archive/ Corbis; pp. 10–11, 38–39 Originally published in Historical Atlas of the World, © J. W. Cappelens Forlag A/S, Oslo, 1962. Maps by Berit Lie. Used with permission of J. W. Cappelens Forlag; p. 12 Ashmolean Museum, University of Oxford, UK/Bridgeman Art Library; pp. 12 (inset), 46, 64; Bildarchiv Preussischer Kulturbesitz/Art Resource, NY; p. 14 Louvre, Paris, France/Bridgeman Art Library; pp. 16–17 Archives Larousse, Paris, France, Lauros/Giraudon/Bridgeman Art Library; pp. 17, 28, 58, 85, 95, 96; Erich Lessing/Art Resource, NY; p. 20 akg-images/ Schuetze/Rodemann; p. 23 Giradaun/Bridgeman Art Library; p. 24 akg-images/FranÁois Guenet; p. 27 Alinari/Art Resource, NY; p. 30 HIP/Art Resource, NY; p.33 © Gian Berto Vanni/Corbis; p. 41 Private Collection, Archives Charmet/Bridgeman Art Library; p. 44 The Art Archive/ Bodleian Library Oxford; pp. 49, 56, 59 Réunion des Musées Nationaux/ Art Resource, NY; pp. 60, 80 Scala/Art Resource, NY; p. 67 Nimatallah/ Art Resource, NY; p. 84 Giraudon/Art Resource, NY; p. 86 akg-images; p. 91 Cameraphoto/Art Resource, NY; p. 92 Guildhall Art Gallery, Corporation of London, UK/Bridgeman Art Library; p. 98 NASA Kennedy Space Center.

Designer: Tahara Anderson
Photo Researcher: Jeffrey Wendt